بِسْمِ اللّٰهِ الرَّحْمٰنِ الرَّحِيمِ

In the name of God, most Gracious, most Merciful

AL
MAHDI

and
the End of Time

Muhammad ibn 'Izzat
Muhammad 'Arif

DAR AL TAQWA

© Dar Al Taqwa Ltd. 1997

Al-Mahdi - First Published 1997
          - Second Edition 2007

ISBN 1-870582-75-6

Translation: Aisha Bewley

Editor: Abdalhaqq Bewley

Production: Bookwork, Norwich

Published by:
    Dar Al Taqwa Ltd.
    7A Melcombe Street
    Baker Street
    London NW1 6AE

Printed & Bound by: Deluxe Printers, London NW10 7NR

Table of Contents

In the name of Allah, the All-Merciful, the Compassionate

"Allah has promised those of you who believe and do right actions that He will make them the successors in the land, as He made those before them successors, and will firmly establish for them their deen, *with which He is pleased, and give them in place of their fear security. 'They worship Me, not attributing any partner to Me.' Any who reject after that, such people are the wantonly deviant."* (24:55)

The Prophet, may Allah bless him and grant him peace, said:

"This affair will reach everything reached by night and day and there will not remain a single house of mud or hair which Allah will not cause this *deen* to enter, whether by the might of a mighty man or the humility of a humble man, a might by which Allah will exalt Islam and a humility by which He will humiliate disbelief."

(Related by Ahmad, at-Tabarani, al-Hakim, Ibn Hibban and al-Hafiz al-Muqaddasi)

1

Preface

Praise belongs to Allah. We praise Him and ask for His forgiveness and His guidance. We seek refuge in Allah from the evils in ourselves and our bad actions. Whomever Allah guides no one can misguide. Whomever He misguides no one can guide. I testify that there is no god but Allah alone with no partner, and I testify that Muhammad is His slave and Messenger.

The most truthful speech is the Book of Allah and the best guidance is the guidance of Muhammad, may Allah bless him and grant him peace. The worst of matters are the new ones. Every bad innovation is misguidance and every misguidance is in the Fire.

"O you who believe! Show fear of Allah with the fear He merits and do not die except as Muslims." (3:103)

"O Mankind! Show fear of your Lord who created you from a single self and created its mate from it and then disseminated many men and women from the two of them. Fear Allah in Whose name you make demands on one another and also fear Him in respect of your families. Allah watches over you continually." (4:1)

"O you who believe! Show fear of Allah and speak words which hit the mark. He will make your actions right for you and forgive you your wrong deeds. Whoever obeys Allah and His Messenger has won a mighty victory."
(33:70-71)

Tyrants live in perpetual fear at the thought of the Mahdi and they will tremble and will swiftly prostrate themselves when he suddenly appears, especially as they are expecting him to arrive at

3

any moment anywhere in the world because their soothsayers have warned them of his imminent arrival. He will be the precursor of the victory of the Truth and the fall of all tyrants. He heralds the end of injustice and oppression and the beginning of the final rising of the sun of Islam which will never again set and which will ensure the happiness and elevation of mankind. This book brings the good news that the Mahdi is one of Allah's clear signs whose truth will soon be made evident to everyone.

Divine Justice obliges Allah Almighty to send a man to humanity to put its affairs in order after they have been corrupted and when injustice and misery have become widespread. This man will eventually come as a token of Allah's compassion for His slaves to give them the opportunity to repent, so that the corrupt may be distinguished from the good and those who strive from those who hang back. It is part of the Divine Wisdom which will complete the history of humanity. The Mahdi will come to confront the Dajjal, the False Messiah, after the Jews' final ascendancy.

There have been many who have claimed to be the Mahdi over the course of history, and many of the enemies of Islam among the Jews, Christians and pagans will also make this claim, so that they can confuse the community and make them lose confidence in the true Mahdi, to the point that people will say that there is no Mahdi at all.

One aspect of Allah's bounty, however, is that before the Mahdi appears there will appear certain clear signs. He will have certain traits and unique characteristics which do not exist in anyone else. True Muslims will recognise them and not be deceived. All Muslims should prepare to welcome the awaited man, this trustworthy and truthful youth from the east, the Mahdi supported by Heaven. Beware of those who falsely claim to be him. They are either Antichrists wearing the garments of righteous men or advance troops from the army of those who worship the Dajjal, the enemies of Allah.

This book is simply an attempt to make it absolutely clear that the Mahdi is a reality so that persecuted exiles may be certain that Allah will give victory to His *deen* through a man of this community and rejoice that relief is on the way; and so that the enemies of

4

Allah may know that 'Allah will perfect His Light, even though the idolaters hate it,' and that the state of falsehood will not abide and the state of the Truth is eternal.

> *"So let those who sell the life of this world for the Next World fight in the way of Allah. If someone fights in the way of Allah, whether he is killed or is victorious, We will pay him an enormous wage. Why should you not fight in the way of Allah, and on behalf of those men, women and children who are oppressed and say, 'Our Lord, take us out of this city whose inhabitants are wrongdoers! Give us a protector from You! Give us a helper from You!'"* (4:75)

Allah is greater! There is no conqueror but Allah! Praise be to Allah, the Lord of the worlds!

May Allah bless our master Muhammad and his family and Companions and grant them abundant peace.

The poor servant of Allah awaiting the Day of Salvation

Abu'l-Fida' Muhammad ibn 'Izzat Muhammad 'Arif

Chapter One

Evidence in the Qur'an and the *Sunna* for the Reality of the Mahdi

Qur'anic evidence

Some commentators report that the Mahdi is alluded to in Allah's words:

> *"They will have disgrace in this world and in the Next World they will have a terrible punishment."* (2:114)

At-Tabari said regarding the words *"They will have disgrace in this world"* that as-Suddi said that their disgrace in this world will come about when the Mahdi comes and Constantinople is conquered and he kills them. That is the disgrace referred to. The punishment is of course Hellfire which will never be lightened for its inhabitants, nor will they be killed in it and die.

Al-Qurtubi related from Qatada and as-Suddi that *"disgrace in this world"* refers to the advent of the Mahdi and the conquest of various great cities of the unbelievers. Ibn Kathir, as-Suddi, 'Ikrima and Wa'il ibn Da'ud explained *"disgrace in this world"* as being the emergence of the Mahdi. However, *"disgrace in this world"* bears a more general significance than that. Ash-Shawkani also states in his *tafsir* that their disgrace in his world shall be when the Mahdi emerges and conquers and slays them.

In *Nur al-Absar*, Shaykh Sayyid ash-Shablanji says that Muqatal ibn Sulayman and those commentators who follow him say about the *tafsir* of the *ayat*: *"He is notification of the Hour. Do not have any doubt about it. And follow Me: this is a straight path,"* (43:61) that it refers to the Mahdi who will come at the end of time and that after him the signs of the Last Hour will appear.

Evidence in the *Sunna*

Imam 'Ali, may Allah be pleased with him, said that the Messenger of Allah, may Allah bless him and grant him peace, said, "The Mahdi is one of us, the People of the House. Allah will instate him overnight." (Related by Ibn Majah and Ahmad)

Abu Sa'id al-Khudri said that the Messenger of Allah, may Allah bless him and grant him peace, said, "The Mahdi will be of my stock and will have a broad forehead and a hooked nose. He will fill the earth will equity and justice as it was previously filled with oppression and tyranny, and he will rule for seven years." (Abu Dawud)

Abu Sa'id al-Khudri said that the Messenger of Allah, may Allah bless him and grant him peace, said, "During the last days of my community, the Mahdi will emerge. Allah will give him abundant rain and the earth will bring forth its plants and give forth its wealth and herds will multiply and the community will be huge. He will live for seven or eight years." (al-Hakim)

Umm Salama, may Allah be pleased with her, said that she heard the Messenger of Allah, may Allah bless him and grant him peace, say, "The Mahdi will be from my family, the descendants of Fatima." (Abu Dawud and al-Hakim)

'Abdullah ibn 'Abbas said that the Messenger of Allah, may Allah bless him and grant him peace, declared, "A nation which has me at its beginning, 'Isa ibn Maryam at its end and the Mahdi in between will never be destroyed." (Ahmad, Abu Nu'aym and an-Nasa'i)

Abu Sa'id al-Khudri said that the Messenger of Allah, may Allah bless him and grant him peace, said, "The Last Hour will not come until the earth is filled with injustice and oppression. Then a man of my family (or of the People of my House) will arise and fill it with justice and equity as it was previously filled with injustice and oppression." (Ahmad, Ibn Hibban, al-Hakim, and Abu Nu'aym)

8

Abu Mas'ud said that the Prophet, may Allah bless him and grant him peace, said, "If there were only a single day of this world left, Allah would lengthen it until He sent a man from me or my family whose name is the same as mine and whose father's name is the same as my father's." (Abu Dawud and at-Tirmidhi)

Abu Umama said, "The Messenger of Allah, may Allah bless him and grant him peace, spoke to us and mentioned the Dajjal and said, 'Madina expels corruption as bellows expel the impurity of iron.' He called that day the 'Day of Purification'. Umm Sharik asked, 'Where will the Arabs be on that day, Messenger of Allah?' He said, 'They will be few on that day. Most of them will be in Jerusalem and their Imam will be the Mahdi, a righteous man. One day during the time that their Imam is the Mahdi, 'Isa ibn Maryam will descend as he steps forward to lead them in the Dawn Prayer. The Imam will step back so that 'Isa can go forward but he will place his hand between his shoulders and say to him, "You go forward. The *iqama* was said for you." So their Imam will lead them in the prayer.'" (al-Hakim, Ibn Majah, Ibn Khuzayma and Abu Nu'aym)

According to Abu Hurayra, the Prophet, may Allah bless him and grant him peace, said. "The Mahdi will remain in my community for at least seven, or perhaps eight or nine years. In those years my community will enjoy a time of happiness such as they have never experienced before. Heaven will send down rain upon them in torrents, the earth will not withhold any of its plants, and wealth will be available to all. A man will stand and say, 'Give to me, Mahdi!' and he will say, 'Take.'" (at-Tabarani)

Jabir reported that the Messenger of Allah, may Allah bless him and grant him peace, said, "'Isa ibn Maryam will descend and their amir, the Mahdi, will say, 'Come and lead us in the prayer.' He will say, 'No, you are amirs of one another,' as a mark of honour from Allah to this community." (al-Harith ibn Abi Usama)

'Abdullah ibn 'Abbas reported that the Messenger of Allah, may Allah bless him and grant him peace, said, "The Mahdi is the peacock of the people of the Garden." (ad-Daylami)

Abu Ayyub al-Ansari stated that the Messenger of Allah, may Allah bless him and grant him peace, said to Fatima, "Our Prophet is the best of Prophets and he is your father. Our martyr is the best of martyrs and he is your father's uncle, Hamza. Among us is one who has two wings on which he flies wherever he wishes in the Garden. He is your father's cousin, Ja'far. Among us are the two grandsons of this community, al-Hasan and al-Husayn, who are your sons, and of our lineage will be the Mahdi." (at-Tabarani)

'Abdullah ibn Safwan reported that Umm Salama said that the Messenger of Allah, may Allah bless him and grant him peace, said, "People who have no protection (i.e. the oppressed) or provision or equipment will take refuge in this House. An army will be sent against them and while they are in the desert the earth will swallow them up." (Muslim)

'Ali reported that the Messenger of Allah, may Allah bless him and grant him peace, said, "A man will emerge from Transoxiana called al-Harith ibn Harrath, in whose vanguard there will be a man called Mansur who will prepare the way for and empower the family of Muhammad, may Allah bless him and grant him peace, as Quraysh empowered the Messenger of Allah, may Allah bless him and grant him peace. It is obligatory for every believer to help him (or respond to him)." (Abu Dawud, an-Nasa'i and al-Bayhaqi)

'Abdullah ibn 'Abbas reported that the Messenger of Allah, may Allah bless him and grant him peace, said, "There have been four great kings on the earth: two were believers and two unbelievers. The believers were Dhu'l-Qarnayn and Sulayman, and the unbelievers were Nimrod and Bakhtinasr. There will be a fifth king, from the People of my House." (Ibn al-Jawzi)

Ka'b al-Ahbar said, "I find the Mahdi recorded in the books of the Prophets. There will be no injustice or oppression under his rule." (ad-Dani)

Umm Salama said, "Once when the Messenger of Allah, may Allah bless him and grant him peace, was lying down in my room he sat up saying, 'We belong to Allah and to Him we return.' I asked, 'By my father and mother, why did you say that, may Allah bless you and grant you peace?' He said, 'An army of my community will come from the direction of Syria making for the House against a man whom Allah will defend from them until they are in the desert beyond Dhu'l-Hulayfa, where the earth will swallow them up. They will meet differing fates.' I said, 'Messenger of Allah, will the earth swallow all of them if their fates differ?' He said, 'Among them will be people who are compelled. Among them will be people who are compelled,' three times." (Ahmad, Abu Ya'la and al-Haythami)

Chapter Two

Statements by Scholars about the Reality of the Mahdi

Ibn Taymiyya said, "The *hadiths* used as a proof of the coming of the Mahdi are sound and related by Abu Dawud, at-Tirmidhi, Ahmad and others from Ibn Mas'ud and others." (*Minhaj as-Sunna* 4:211)

Imam al-Bayhaqi says, "The *hadiths* about the emergence of the Mahdi have sound *isnads* and make it clear that he will be from the family of the Prophet."

Ibn Kathir states in *an-Nihaya al-Bidaya wa'n-Nihaya*, "The Mahdi will come at the end of time. He will be one of the Rightly-guided Caliphs and guided Imams and he is not the one for whom the Rafidites [Shi'a] wait, expecting him to emerge from underground in Samarra. That has no basis or source or authentic provenance."

Ibn al-Jawziyya says in *Ighatha al-Lahfan*, "The Muslims are waiting for the descent of the Messiah 'Isa ibn Maryam from heaven, when he will break the crosses, kill the pigs and kill his enemies among the Jews and the Christian who worship him. They are waiting for the Mahdi to emerge from the House of the Prophet and fill the earth with justice as it is now filled with injustice."

Al-Kattani, as-Sijistani and others mention that the *hadiths* about the Mahdi have multiple lines of transmission and are therefore reliable.

Ash-Shawkani said, "The *hadiths* related about the Mahdi which can be relied on number fifty, some being sound, some good and some weak. They are transmitted without any doubt. Indeed many *hadiths* of lesser weight are categorised as being transmitted by multiple chains of transmission. The Traditions which deal with the Mahdi are also numerous and direct."

In his book, *ash-Shu'a*, Qadi 'Iyad mentions the signs of the Hour, which include the emergence of the Mahdi.

People's positions regarding the Mahdi

People can be basically divided into three groups regarding the way they view the Mahdi.

1. The people of intellectual analysis

These are the people who rely on theoretical philosophy and logical analysis for their conclusion without bothering with proper research and scholarly effort. They reject anything that disagrees with their ideas as being beyond their experience. They dismiss all reports and traditions reported about this matter, even if they have sound chains of transmission, simply because there have been charlatans and deceivers who have claimed to be the Mahdi. At the forefront of these are Ahmad Amin in his book, *The Dawn of Islam*, and Sa'd Muhammad Hasan in his book, *The Idea of the Mahdi in Islam*. This position is false because it relies on reason alone and has no sound scholarly basis.

2. The positions of the esoterists and the Shi'a

These are the people who agree about the Mahdi but who transmit reports about him which are totally without foundation. They believe that he is Muhammad ibn al-Hasan al-'Askari who was born and then disappeared and is now hidden underground, and that no one knows when he will emerge. This position is not tenable because it is based on suppositions and delusions.

3. The position of the people of the *Sunna* and the Community

These are the people who rely on the sound and firm transmissions with proper *isnads* originating from the Messenger of Allah, may Allah bless him and grant him peace, and from the Companions and Followers, and which are founded on proof and evidence which is not incompatible with reason and sound logic. At the forefront of these are Imam Ahmad ibn Hanbal, Ibn Taymiyya, Ibn Kathir, as-Suyuti, Ibn Hajar, and others.

Nasir ad-Din al-Albani says in describing people's deviant fews regarding the Mahdi:

"They include those who know that what is related from the common people is superstition and think at the same time that such superstition is an inseparable part of belief in the coming of the Mahdi. For this reason they deny the Mahdi altogether, taking the position of someone who "throws out the baby with the bath water". This is similar to the Mu'tazilites who denied the reality of the Decree because they saw a group of Muslims who espoused absolute predestination. In doing so they denied an essential tenet of faith.

"Some of them have seen that throughout the course of Islamic history the idea of the Mahdi has been badly abused on many occasions and has been exploited by many self-interested persons and deluded visionaries and that in its name many unjustifiable seditions have taken place, the last of them being the recent conflict in the Haram of Makka. They think that by denial of the Mahdi the cause of these troubles will be eradicated. "

The *hadith* "There is no Mahdi but 'Isa" is forged

This *hadith* is related by Ibn Majah and al-Hakim from Ibn 'Abbas, may Allah be pleased with him and says: "There is no Mahdi except 'Isa, peace be upon him."

Al-Hakim said that this *hadith* does not constitute evidence. As-San'ani said that it is a forged *hadith*. Adh-Dhahabi said that it is contradicted elsewhere. Ibn Taymiyya stated that it is weak, as did al-Bayhaqi, al-Haythami and Ibn al-Qayyim.

Al-Qurtubi observes in his famous *tafsir*, "The *hadiths* from the Prophet, may Allah bless him and grant him peace, regarding the emergence of the Mahdi as being from his family from the descendants of Fatima are firm and sounder than this *hadith*. One does not judge by it."

The Mahdi in the Books of the Jews and Christians

Ka'b al-Ahbar said: "I find the Mahdi recorded in the books of the Prophets. There will be no injustice or oppression in his rule."

For instance the Book of Revelation says: "And I saw and behold a white horse. He that sat on him ... went forth conquering and to conquer." (6:2) Later it says: "Then I looked and saw a man standing on the mount Sion, and with him an hundred forty and four thousand, having his name and his father's name written in their foreheads." (14:1)

It is clear that this man is the Mahdi who will ride a white horse and judge by the Qur'an (with justice) and with whom will be men with the marks of prostration on their foreheads.

That is supported in the same text in Chapter 12:1-5 which speaks about the origin of this noble man: "There appeared a great wonder in heaven: a woman clothed with the sun, and the moon under her feet, and upon her head a crown of twelve stars. ... And she brought forth a man child, who was to rule all nations with a rod of iron." The description of this extraordinary woman clearly indicates Fatima az-Zahra from whose descendants will come the Mahdi.

Why he will be called 'Mahdi'

Ka'b al-Ahbar says, "He will be called 'Mahdi' because he will guide (*yahdi*) to something hidden and will bring out the Torah and Gospel from a town called Antioch." (Abu Nu'aym)

As-Suyuti mentioned in *al-Hawi* that the Messenger of Allah, may Allah bless him and grant him peace, said, "He is called the Mahdi because he will guide people to a mountain in Syria from which he will bring out the volumes of the Torah to refute the Jews. At the hands of the Mahdi the Ark of the Covenant will be brought forth at Lake Tiberias and taken and placed in Jerusalem."

Ad-Dani said that he is called the Mahdi because he will be guided to a mountain in Syria from which he will bring forth the volumes of the Torah with which to argue against the Jews and at his hands a group of them will become Muslim.

Sulayman ibn 'Isa said, "I have heard that it is at the hands of the Mahdi that the Ark of the Covenant will be brought from Lake Tiberias and will be carried and placed before him in Jerusalem. When the Jews see it, they will become Muslim except for a few of them."

In general, 'Mahdi' is the name of something which is guided. It designates someone whom Allah will guide to guidance, make firm in it, and support with armies. He will guide the community to the path of might, right and firmness. May Allah makes us guided guides! He will be called thus, and his real name will be Muhammad ibn 'Abdullah and his *kunya* Abu 'Abdullah. Allah will institute him – that is, guide him – in one night, and he will be the Mahdi. Allah knows best.

His physical description

Abu Ja'far ibn 'Ali al-Baqir said, "Imam 'Ali, may Allah be pleased with him, was asked about the physical appearance of the Mahdi and said, 'He is a well-built youth with a handsome face whose hair reaches his shoulders. The light of his face is contrasted by the darkness of his hair and beard.'"

Muhammad as-Safarini said in his book, *The False Messiah and the secrets of the Last Hour*, "He is described as being brown-skinned, a slender man of medium height, with a broad forehead, a high, hooked nose, finely arched eyebrows, clear, dark eyes, white teeth with gaps between them, and slightly bow-legged. One transmission states that he is a little slow of speech. When he is delayed, he will strike his left thigh with his right hand. He will be forty, although one variant says that he will be between thirty and forty. He will humble towards Allah."

Chapter Three
The Signs Accompanying the Mahdi

The Signs which will precede him

Traditions clearly relate that there will be various signs before the appearance of the Mahdi. Many reports specify civil wars, calamities and other signs which precede him. Whenever it is thought that these troubles have come to an end, they will start up again and spread and intensify until there is no Arab house they do not enter and no Muslim they do not affect. There will be violent deaths, intense disputes and general affliction to the point that the living will envy the dead. A huge fire will appear from the east which can be seen in the sky a distance of three days' journey away. Sixty liars will arise, each of whom will claim to be sent by Allah. One of the towns of Syria will be swallowed up by the earth and a star will rise in the east which will be as luminous as the moon. Redness will appear in the sky. There are many other specific signs mentioned in Tradition.

- A black wind will arise and there will be earthquakes in which many will be killed.

- The water of the Euphrates will flood Kufa and ruin it.

- There will be a call from heaven to all the people of the earth and everyone will hear it in their own language and people responsible for innovations will be transmogrified.

- Slaves will cease to obey their masters.

- A voice in the middle night of Ramadan will awaken sleepers and alarm those who are awake.

- There will be tumult in Shawwal, war and fighting in Dhu'l-Qa'da, and the plundering of the *Hajjis* in Dhu'l-Hijja.

- There will be such slaughter that blood runs in the streets.

- Sacred things will be violated in the Haram.

- A marvel will occur between Jumada and Rajab.

- There will be much slaughter and it will last for a long time. A third of mankind will be killed and a third will die, and those in authority will be tyrants. People will be believers in the evening and unbelievers by the morning.

- The Turks will come forth and descend on the Arabian peninsula and armies will be mustered and the caliph killed.

- Distress will be intense and a caller will call out on the walls of Damascus: "Woe to the Arabs for an evil which has drawn near!"

Following the occurrence of these signs the Imam al-Mahdi will emerge and rally his forces to help this community to remove their distress, through his sincere desire to rid the lands from domination of the impious, sinful people who rule them. He will defend all righteous people against the unbelievers and tyrants. His troops will be victorious and the people of the heavens and earth, birds and wild animals will rejoice in his rule.

Signs announcing his imminent appearance

The rapid passing of time

Who among us is now able to be truly aware of the blessing of the moment? By Allah, each day comes to an end and it is as if we have spent its hours in a dream. Time is passing so swiftly that it seems as though a day lasts only an hour. Al-Khattabi said, "The Last Hour will not come before time contracts, a year being like a month, a month like a week, a week like a day, a day like an hour, and an hour like the burning of a palm leaf." It is said that that will happen in the time of the Mahdi or 'Isa or both.

There is no doubt that many of the signs foretelling the Mahdi and 'Isa have already appeared. This also means the return of the Nation of the Qur'an and the end of the hidden Masonic Jewish rule which oppresses all nations in the world today and which itself dances to the tune of the Antichrist.

The eclipse of the Moon in Ramadan

Abu Nu'aym relates in *al-Fitan* that Sharik said, "It has reached me that before the Mahdi emerges the moon will be eclipsed twice in Ramadan."

Shaykh Mar'i looked into this, since normally the moon is only eclipsed on the nights when it is full and the sun on the days when the moon is invisible.

This is a sign which will disgrace every pretender. If this extraordinary cosmic sign does not precede someone who claims to be the Mahdi, he will be known to be a false liar and if it does happen that there are two lunar eclipses in the month of Ramadan of any year, it will certainly mean that it is the year of the appearance of the man for whom the world is waiting, the man against whom no one will have power. The tyrants will tremble when they hear of him because they know that he is the awaited conqueror, may Allah enlist us in his army!

The war in the Gulf and the Europeans

The Prophet, may Allah bless him and grant him peace, said, "A man of the Umayyads will take power in Egypt and then his power will be taken from him, or wrested from him, and he will flee to Byzantium and enlist them against the people of Islam; and that will be the first of the battles." (at-Tabarani)

The word Egypt normally means the land of the Pharaohs, as the Almighty says:

"We revealed to Musa and his brother: 'Settle your people in houses in Egypt and make your houses places of worship and establish the prayer and give good news to the believers.'" (10:87)

But in this *hadith* the word can mean any land. It may well indicate what happened in the Gulf war. Saddam provoked the Gulf War. Allah knows best, but I believe it to be the first of the civil wars marking the end of time.

The star with the tail

Ka'b al-Ahbar said, "A star with a luminous tail will rise from the East before the Mahdi emerges." Some people say that when this star with a tail appears, there will be catastrophes and disasters for the Jews and Christians. This is why they consider it an evil sign. They call it Halley's Comet after its discoverer. It is a star which has existed since before recorded history and has a particular orbit in which it moves. When it passes the earth during its orbit, its luminous tail appears.

According to Ibn Kathir, Ibn 'Abbas said, "I did not sleep last night at all." When he was asked why, he said, "They said that a star with a tail had appeared and I feared that the Smoke would spread." One variant has "...that the Dajjal would appear. It is known that Dajjal and the Mahdi will be alive at the same time. So I did not sleep all night." Ibn Kathir added that the Smoke is one of the awaited signs. The Almighty says:

"Be on the watch then for a day when the sky exhibits a distinctive smoke which will cover the people. This is a painful punishment." (44:11)

There is no doubt that the 'distinctive smoke' is one of the major signs of the Last Hour, like the Beast and the rising of the sun from the west. When a true Muslim sees a wondrous cosmic sign like a star with a tail, he immediately fears that the sign of the Smoke will follow it, after which there will be no asking for respite. We ask Allah for safety and well-being!

The words of the Qur'an, *"be on the watch"* means we should watch out for Halley's comet every time it comes into orbit. Halley did not really discover it. People knew about it long before him and watched out for it as well. It draws near to earth every 86 years. Its tail extends for thirty million kilometres and is composed of smoke and dust. It appeared at the birth of 'Isa and at the birth of our master Muhammad, may Allah bless him and grant him peace; and also on the day when Constantinople was conquered by Muhammad al-Fatih. Because of this the Europeans consider it an evil omen for them. It will also appear when the Mahdi comes, when once more the unbelievers will be terrified.

The Mosque of the Prophet will be like a white fortress

The Prophet said, "The Day of Deliverance! What is the Day of Deliverance?" They said, "Messenger of Allah, what is the Day of Deliverance?" He said, "The Dajjal will come and look at Madina and will say to his Companions, 'Do you see this white fortress? This is the Mosque of Ahmad.'" (Related by Ahmad and al-Hakim)

Glory be to Allah! This concerns the mosque of the Prophet which now looks like a fortress. That has happened by Allah's decree to fulfil the prophecy of the Best of Mankind, the Truthful Confirmed One, may Allah bless him and grant him peace.

Spitting in faces

The Messenger of Allah, may Allah bless him and grant him peace, said, "The Mahdi will not emerge until people spit in each other's faces." (Nu'aym ibn Hammad, *al-Hawi*)

22

I have heard that certain despots had an argument in a summit conference which reached the point where they cursed each other and one of them stood up and spat in the face of the other. This is because they do not judge by what Allah has revealed:

"In it We prescribed for them: a life for a life, an eye for an eye, a nose for a nose, an ear for an ear, a tooth for a tooth, and retaliation for wounds. But if anyone forgoes it as sadaqa, it shall be an expiation for him. Any who do not judge by what Allah has revealed, such people are wrong-doers." (5:11)

Allah also says:

"The people of the Gospel should judge by what Allah revealed in it. Those who do not judge by what Allah has revealed are wanton deviants." (5:47)

The leaders of secular republics and Masonic governments are enemies of Allah, even if they have Muslim names.

"You consider them united but their hearts are far apart." (59:14)

This is why Allah has given some of them power over others and has abased and humiliated them. So they spit in each other's faces because they do not judge or rule by the Law of the Sustainer of the heavens and the earth, the King of kings. In reality, they are following the Masonic code as enemies of Allah.

The profanation of the Sacred House and the destruction of the Arabs

Abu Hurayra reported that the Messenger of Allah, may Allah bless him and grant him peace, said, "A man will be given allegiance [at the Ka'ba] between the Corner [of the Ka'ba] and the *Maqam Ibrahim*. The House will only be profaned by its own people. When they profane it, do not ask about the destruction of the Arabs. Then the Ethiopians will come and ruin it so that it will never again be inhabited. They are people who will seek to take out its treasure." (Ahmad and Abu Dawud)

The Sacred House was profaned in our own time in 1400 H in an internecine conflict. We seek refuge with Allah! Blood was spilt in the courtyard of the Haram and it was claimed that Muhammad 'Abdullah al-Qahtani was the Mahdi. His followers carried weapons in spite of the fact that they knew that the Mahdi will appear suddenly and will come from a house in the vicinity of Safa and will only accept people's allegiance under compulsion. They also knew that he must be preceded by signs like the comet and the slaughter at Mina and other established signs such as the army being swallowed up in the desert, none of which had happened. Woe indeed to anyone who profanes the Sanctuary of Allah through crime, rebellion, lies or aggression! The Almighty says:

"Those who reject and bar access to the Way of Allah and to the Sacred Mosque which We have appointed for all mankind – equally for those who live near it and those who come from far away – those who desire to profane it with wrongdoing, We shall make them taste a painful punishment." (22:25)

Ibn 'Abbas reported that the Messenger of Allah, may Allah bless him and grant him peace, said, "The three people most hated by Allah are: a person who deviates from right conduct in the *Haram* (sanctuaries of Makka and Madina); a person who follows the traditions of the pre-Islamic Time of Ignorance; and a person who seeks to shed somebody's blood without any legal right." (al-Bukhari)

He also said, "It is not lawful for anyone to carry weapons in Makka." (Muslim) That is because doing so will cause fear to the Muslims. Makka is a place which must be safe and in which people must have security, safety, peace and tranquillity. It is a place in which it is unlawful even to carry weapons, let alone use them,

24

and it is absolutely unlawful to profane the sanctity of the Ancient House in any way. Whoever does so has become a deviant.

Ibn 'Abbas reported that the Messenger of Allah, may Allah bless him and grant him peace, said, "Allah made this city inviolable on the day when He created the heavens and the earth, and it will be inviolable by Allah's Sanctity until the Day of Rising. Fighting within it was not lawful for anyone before me and it was only made lawful for me for one hour of one day. It is inviolable by a ban imposed by Allah until the Day of Resurrection." (al-Bukhari)

The present situation shows the nearness of his coming

Abu Ja'far Muhammad ibn 'Ali, may Allah be pleased with him, said, "The Mahdi will only appear at a time when people are experiencing great fear and are afflicted by disturbances and civil war and other disasters. Before that there will be a plague, much slaughter among the Arabs, intense disputes between people, dispersion in the *deen* and frequent changes of ruler, to such an extent that people will long for death morning and evening due to the rapacious greed they see in others and the way people devour one another. He will emerge when there is hopelessness and despair about there being any escape. How happy is the one who joins him and is one of his helpers! Woe to the one who opposes him and resists him!"

Plundering *Hajjis*, inter-tribal fighting, and slaughter at Mina

'Amr ibn Shu'ayb reported from his grandfather that the Messenger of Allah, may Allah bless him and grant him peace, said, "In Dhu'l-Qa'da the tribes will fight. The *Hajjis* will be looted and there will be a battle at Mina in which many will be slain and blood will flow until it runs over the Jamra al-'Aqaba and until their companion flees to a point between the Corner and the *Maqam* and is forced to accept people's allegiance. He is told, 'If you refuse, we will cut off your head.' As many people will pledge allegiance to him as fought at Badr and the inhabitants of the heaven and earth will be pleased with them."

Abu Yusuf said that 'Abdullah ibn 'Amr said, "People will perform *hajj* together and gather without an Imam. While they are camped, they will be afflicted by something like rabies. The tribes will attack one another and fight until 'Aqaba runs with blood. They will turn to the best man of them and go to him while he is pressing his face to the Ka'ba weeping – I can visualise his tears – and say, 'Come and let us pledge allegiance to you.' He will say 'Woe to you! How many treaties you have broken and how much blood you have shed!' But he will be forced to accept their allegiance. If you meet him, give him your allegiance. He is the Mahdi on earth and the Mahdi in heaven." (al-Hakim and Nu'aym ibn Hammad)

Injustice and tyrannical rule will cover the earth

Abu Sa'id al-Khudri said, "The Messenger of Allah, may Allah bless him and grant him peace, mentioned an affliction which will befall this community in which no one will find any refuge from injustice. He said, 'Allah will send a man from my family and he will fill the earth with justice and equity as it was previously filled with injustice and tyranny. The inhabitants of the heavens and the inhabitants of the earth will be pleased with him and such plants will be produced by the earth that the living will wish the dead could come back to life (when they see the security, happiness, and blessing of the earth and the might of Islam.) That will last for about seven or eight years.'" (at-Tabarani and Abu Nu'aym)

Hudhayfa reported that he heard the Messenger of Allah, may Allah bless him and grant him peace, say, "Woe to this community from tyrannical rulers! How they will kill and terrorise godfearing people, except for those who appear to obey them! Some godfearing believers will pretend to co-operate with them with their tongues but flee from them in their hearts. When Allah Almighty wants to restore the power of Islam, he will crush every stubborn tyrant. He has the power to do whatever He wishes to put the community right after its corruption." He continued, may Allah bless him and grant him peace, "Hudhayfa, if there only remained a single day of this world, Allah would lengthen that day until a man from the people of my house was given control over it. Battles will take place under his command and Islam will be victorious. Allah does not break His promise and He is swift at the Reckoning." (Abu Nu'aym and al-Isfahani)

The rescuing group

Mu'adh ibn Jabal reported that the Messenger of Allah, may Allah bless him and grant him peace, said, "A group of my community will continue to fight for the Truth and overcome those who resist them until the last of them fights the False Messiah." (Agreed on by al-Bukhari and Muslim)

This *hadith* confirms the continuity of the Muslim community from the time of the Messenger of Allah, may Allah bless him and grant him peace. This continuity is evidence for the continuous existence of the Party of the Truth until the last of them fights the False Messiah – what is meant by the last of them is the Mahdi and those Muslims who are with him – until 'Isa ibn Maryam returns and kills the false Messiah at the Ludd Gate in Palestine.

Let us reflect on the words of the Prophet, may Allah bless him and grant him peace, "They will continue to fight for the Truth and overcome those who resist them." These are people who will uphold the creed of truth and act according to it, fighting to make the Word of Allah uppermost. They will overcome those who resist them by their knowledge, eloquence and *jihad*. They are the victorious Party of the Truth; but they are people whose presence is not recognised and whose absence is not missed.

This period in question is the time of exile and testing and these people will prepare the way for the coming of the Mahdi, may Allah be pleased with him. Their hallmark will be that they are Muslims who act by the Book of Allah and the *Sunna* of His Messenger, may Allah bless him and grant him peace, secretly and openly, not fearing the blame of any critic. They reject idols and judge in disputes between them according to what Allah has sent down and they strive with truthfulness, constancy and sincerity for the return of the Caliphate.

Despair about the coming of the Mahdi

'Abdullah ibn 'Abbas said, "Allah Almighty will send the Mahdi after despair has reached the point that people will say, 'There is no Mahdi.' Three hundred and fifteen of the people of Syria, the same as the number of the Muslim warriors at Badr, will go to him from Syria and bring him out of the valley of Makka from a house at as-Safa. They will force him to accept their allegiance and he will lead them in the two *rak'ats* of the traveller's prayer at the Maqam and then will mount the minbar." (Nu'aym ibn Hammad)

Although this *hadith* is considered weak because its chain of transmission includes al-Walid ibn Muslim who is a forger according to the people of knowledge, its meaning is in accordance with other *hadiths* on the same subject. The Mahdi will come to mankind at a time when there is much cruelty and tyranny and despotic rule, when the community is heedless and negligent, and when corruption has become widespread, as we see now. People will despair and say, "There is no Mahdi." And indeed this is what we have heard from many people.

The situation will worsen until, as you will see, no one will dare mention the Mahdi from the minbar. Few speak about him now. This is proof of cowardice, ignorance and despairing of him. However, the mercy of Allah will reach weary mankind and a youth from the East will arrive–the Mahdi, may Allah be pleased with him. The first of his helpers will be people of Syria, whose number will be that of the Muslim warriors atBadr. They will come to him in Makka and bring him out of a house near Safa.

Chapter Four

The Emergence of the Sufyani and the Dajjal

The emergence of the Sufyani

One of the most conclusive signs of the coming of the Mahdi is the emergence of the Sufyani (descendant of Abu Sufyan) who will precede him. The Sufyani's name will be 'Urwa ibn Muhammad and his *kunya* will be Abu 'Utba. Shaykh Mar'i said: "The Sufyani will be one of the descendants of Khalid ibn Yazid ibn Abi Sufyan, cursed in heaven and on earth. He is the most unjust of the creatures of Allah."

'Ali, may Allah be pleased with him, said, "The Sufyani will be one of the descendants of Khalid ibn Yazid ibn Abi Sufyan: a man with a large head, a pockmarked face, and white spots in his eyes. He will emerge from part of Damascus and most of those who follow him will be from the tribe of Kalb. He will kill to the point of slicing open the bellies of women and slaying their unborn children. A man from the people of my House will come out against him in the Haram. The Sufyani will hear of this and send one of his armies to fight him which he will defeat. Then the Sufyani himself will come against him with his people until he crosses some land in the desert which swallows them up. Only those who are among them under compulsion will be saved." (al-Hakim, *Mustadrak*)

Muhammad ibn as-Samit said, "I asked al-Husayn ibn 'Ali, 'Is there any sign before this business (the emergence of the Mahdi)?' He replied, 'Yes.' I said, 'What is it?' He said, 'The destruction of the Banu 'Abbas, the emergence of the Sufyani and the earth swallowing people up in the desert.' I asked, 'May I be your ransom, I

29

fear that this will take a long time.' He said, 'It is a chain of events which has its own sequence.'"

According to 'Alqama, Ibn Mas'ud said, "The Messenger of Allah, may Allah bless him and grant him peace, told us, "I warn you of seven severe trials which will occur after me: a trial which will come from Madina, a trial in Makka, a trial which will come from Yemen, a trial which will come from Syria, a trial which will come from the East, a trial which will come from the West, and a trial from the valley of Syria, which is the Sufyani."

Ibn Mas'ud said, "Some of us have seen the first of them and some of this community will see the last of them."

Al-Walid ibn 'Ayyash said, "The trial in Madina was that of Talha and az-Zubayr, the trial in Makka was that of 'Abdullah ibn az-Zubayr, the trial of Syria was from the Banu Umayya [the Umayyads], and the trial of the East is from these people." (al-Hakim and Nu'aym)

The amazing power of the Sufyani

Khalid ibn Ma'dan said, "The Sufyani will emerge with three staffs in his hand. Anyone whom he strikes with them will die." (Nu'aym ibn Hammad)

The Sufyani is a man whose trial involves his person, his power, his speed and his fighting. One of his wonders consists of his staffs which kill anyone he strikes with them. Perhaps they are guns or immensely powerful electrical batons or laser emitters or something similar, or perhaps they work by some magical process.

The *hadith* about the Sufyani confirms that he is a tyrant who will spread corruption and crime in the earth immediately before the appearance of the Mahdi. When he hears of his presence in the Haram he will send one of his armies to seize him or kill him, and the Mahdi and those of the army of Allah with him who have given him their allegiance will fight them. They will defeat the army of the Sufyani and that will be the Mahdi's first victory. The Sufyani will learn of that and will be angry and decide to go himself to meet the Mahdi, taking his army of warriors who are leaders in disbelief and who worship him rather than Allah. When they reach the desert Allah will send Jibril to them and the earth will swallow them up.

The Dajjal is the confirmed enemy of the Mahdi

The Dajjal is the obstinate enemy of the Mahdi who is the leader of the Muslims. He only emerges because of the reappearance of the sun of Islam and the return of its brilliant light which will never again be obscured after that day, the Day of Salvation. The Dajjal will be furious when he hears the shouts of "Allah is Greater" and the declaration of the unity of Allah filling the heavens. Finally Islam will return to spread peace in the earth, the false nations will fall, and the banner of truth and justice will be unfurled and the honour of man restored. After that day there will be no more tyranny or enslavement or pagan fervour.

The Dajjal will be defeated, but before that simple people will believe that he is a god who has the power over life and death. It is simply a magical deception but people are deceived by that since it appears to them that the magic is real. Among the believers there will be some who are not deceived. One man will say to the Dajjal, 'I testify that you are the same Dajjal whose description was given to us by the Messenger of Allah, may Allah bless him and grant him peace.' The Dajjal will say to the people, 'If I kill this man and bring him back to life again, will you doubt my claim?' They will say, 'No.' Then the Dajjal will kill that man and bring him back to life. That man will say, 'Now I am even more certain of your identity than I was before.' The Dajjal will want to kill him but will be unable to do so. (Muslim)

What is absolutely clear is that the Dajjal does not in reality give life to anyone, for Allah alone can give life and cause to die. Glory be to Him! No one shares with Him in that. Yet by means of magic the Dajjal produces the illusion that he has killed a man and brought him back to life, in order to entice people. We seek refuge with Allah!

31

The appearance and destruction of the Dajjal

Jabir ibn 'Abdullah reported that the Messenger of Allah, may Allah bless him and grant him peace, said, "The Dajjal will appear while the *deen* is half asleep." After describing the Dajjal, he went on to say, "Then 'Isa the son of Maryam will descend and will call out at dawn, 'O People! what prevents you from going out against this loathsome liar?' They will say, 'This is a sinful man,' and will go forth. 'Isa ibn Maryam will be there, and the prayer will be called and it will be said 'Go forward, O Spirit of Allah.' He will say, 'Let your Imam go forward and lead you in the prayer.' When they have prayed the *Subh* prayer, they will attack the Dajjal. When the liar sees him, he will melt away as salt melts in water." (*Musnad* of Ahmad ibn Hanbal)

'Abdullah ibn 'Amr narrated that the Messenger of Allah, may Allah bless him and grant him peace, said, "The Dajjal will appear in my Community and he will remain for forty." (He could not say whether he meant forty days, forty months or forty years.) "Allah will then send 'Isa ibn Maryam who will resemble 'Urwa ibn Mas'ud. He will seek out the Dajjal and kill him. Then people will live for seven years, during which time there will be no enmity between any two persons. After that Allah will send a cold wind from the direction of Syria. Anyone on the face of the earth who has a grain of good or faith in them will die. Even if some among you were to go inside a mountain, this wind would reach them and make them die."

He said, "I heard the Messenger of Allah say, may Allah bless him and grant him peace, 'Only evil people will remain and they will be as careless as birds with the characteristics of beasts. They will not recognise what is good or object to evil. Then Shaytan will come to them in human form and say: "Won't you respond?" They will reply, "What do you command us to do?" He will command them to worship idols and they will have abundant provision and comfortable lives. Then the Trumpet will be blown and whoever hears it will hearken to it and raise his hands. The first one to hear it will be someone who is busy mending a cistern for watering his camels. He will faint and other people will also faint. Then

Allah will send, or will cause to be sent, rain which will be like dew and from which the bodies of people will be re-formed.

'Then there will be another blast and they will stand up and look. Then it will be said, "O people, go to your Lord!" They will be made to stand there and they will be questioned. Then it will be said, "Bring out the party of the Fire!" It will be asked, "How many?" The reply will come, "Nine hundred and ninety-nine out of every thousand." That will be the day that will make children white-haired and that will be the day about which Allah has said, *"On the day when the thigh will be uncovered."*'" (Ahmad, *Musnad*)

Abu Umama al-Bahili said, "The Messenger of Allah, may Allah bless him and grant him peace, addressed us and most of his address consisted of a *hadith* in which he told us about the Dajjal and cautioned us. Part of what he said was: 'There will not be a trial on the earth since Allah disseminated the progeny of Adam, peace be upon him, worse than that of the Dajjal. Allah has not sent one Prophet who did not warn his community about him. I am the last of the Prophets and you are the last of the communities, so he must appear among you. If he appears while I am among you, I shall contend with him on behalf of every Muslim, but if he comes when I am not among you, each man must look out for himself and Allah will take care of every Muslim on my behalf. He will appear from the region between Syria and Iraq and will spread mischief right and left. O slaves of Allah, be firm! I will describe him to you with a description not given by any Prophet before me.

'He will appear and say, "I am a Prophet and there is no Prophet after me." Then he will give praise and say, "I am your Lord," but you will not see your Lord until you die. He is one-eyed, and your Lord is not one-eyed. Written between his eyes is "Unbeliever". Every believer, whether literate or illiterate, will be able to read it.

'One aspect of the trial he represents is that he has a garden and a fire. His fire is a garden and his garden a fire. Whoever is tested by his fire should seek refuge with Allah and recite the opening verses of *al-Kahf*: it will become coolness and peace for him as the fire was for Ibrahim. Another aspect is that he will say to a bedouin, "Do you think that if I were to bring your father and mother back to life for you that you would testify that I am your Lord?" He will say, "Yes." So two shaytans will take on the physical form of his father and mother and say, "My son, follow him! He is your Lord."

'Yet another aspect of the trial he represents is that he will have power over someone and kill him and saw him in half with a saw until he is in two halves. Then he will say, "Look at this slave of mine. I will resurrect him now and then he will claim that he has a Lord other than me." So Allah will resurrect him and the foul one will ask him, "Who is your Lord?" He will say, "My Lord is Allah and you are the enemy of Allah. You are the Dajjal. By Allah, I perceive you even more clearly now."'"

Abu Sa'id al-Khudri said that the Messenger of Allah, may Allah bless him and grant him peace, said, "That man will have the highest rank in the Garden of anyone of my Community." Abu Sa'id continued, "By Allah, we used to think that that man could only be 'Umar ibn al-Khattab until he passed away."

He continued, "Another aspect of the trial brought by the Dajjal is that he will order the sky to rain and it will rain, and he will command the earth to grow and it will grow crops. Another aspect is that he will pass by a people who will deny him and all their animals will die. Another is that he will pass a people will believe him and he will command the sky to rain and the earth to flourish, so that on that very evening their herds will become very fat and large with their flanks distended and their udders full of milk. Nothing will remain on the earth which he does not trample underfoot and overcome except for Makka and Madina. When he comes to them through one of their passes, angels with unsheathed swords will confront him until he descends at the red mountain at as-Sabakha. Madina and its inhabitants will be shaken three times and no Hypocrite, man or woman, will remain and not go out to him. In this way the scum will be removed from Madina as the bellows purify iron and that day will be called the Day of Salvation."

Umm Sharik bint Abi Bakr asked, "Messenger of Allah, where will the Arabs be on that day?" He replied, "On that day they will be few in number and most of them will be in Jerusalem. Their Imam will be a righteous man and one day when he is going forward to lead them in the *Subh* prayer, 'Isa ibn Maryam will descend and pray *Subh* with them. Then that Imam will step back to let 'Isa ibn Maryam lead the people in the prayer but 'Isa will put his hand between his shoulders and say, 'Go forward and pray. The *iqama* was said for you.' So their Imam will lead them in the prayer. When he finishes, 'Isa, peace be upon him, will say, 'Open the door!' It will be opened and beyond it will be the Dajjal with 70,000 Jews, all carrying swords and wearing crowns. When the Dajjal looks at 'Isa, he will melt away as salt melts in water and will flee. 'Isa, peace be upon him, will say, 'I have a blow for you the like of which you have never felt before.' He will catch the Dajjal at the eastern gate of al-Ludd and kill him; and Allah will defeat the Jews. Then there will be nothing in Allah's creation which a Jew hides behind which will not be made to speak by Allah, be it stone, tree, wall, animal or tree. It will say, 'O Muslim slave of Allah! Here is a Jew! Come and kill him!"

The Messenger of Allah said, may Allah bless him and grant him peace, "He will live for forty years, and each year will seem like half a year, and then each year will be like a month and each month like a week, and the last of his days will be like flashes. One of you will be at one gate of Madina in the morning and not reach its other gate before evening comes."

He was asked, "Messenger of Allah, how should we pray in those short days?" He said, "Calculate the time of prayer in them the same way as you calculate it in the long days. Then pray."

The Messenger of Allah, may Allah bless him and grant him peace, said, "'Isa ibn Maryam, peace be upon him, will be a just judge in my community and a fair Imam. He will break the crosses and kill the pigs and impose the *jizya,* and *sadaqa* will be abandoned. There will be no striving for sheep or camels. Avarice and enmity will be removed, and the sting of every creature with a sting will be removed so that a child will put his hand in a snake's mouth and it will not harm him and a girl will startle a lion and it will not harm her. A wolf will treat sheep as if it were their dog. The earth will be filled with peace as a vessel is filled with water and there will be complete harmony. Only Allah will be worshipped and war will lay down its burdens and Quraysh will be stripped of its kingdom and the earth will have a silver age. Plants will grow as in the time of Adam, so that a whole group will be satisfied by eating a bunch of grapes and a whole group will be filled by eating a single pomegranate. An ox will be worth such-and-such an amount of property, but a horse will only cost a few dirhams."

They asked, "O Messenger of Allah, why will horses be so cheap?" He said, "They will never be ridden for war." He was asked, "Why will oxen be so expensive?" He replied, "Because all of the earth will be cultivated. There will be three severe years before the Dajjal comes. During them people will experience intense hunger. In the first year Allah will command the sky to withhold a third of its rain and He will command the earth to withhold a third of its plants. Then in the second year He will command the sky to withhold two-thirds of its rain and the earth to withhold two-thirds of its plants. Then in the third year He will command the sky to withhold all its rain and not a drop will fall, and He will command the earth to withhold all its plants. Nothing green will grow. No cloven-hoofed animal will remain alive except what Allah wills." Someone asked, "What will people live on in that time?" He replied, "Saying 'There is no god but Allah,' 'Allah is greater,' 'Glory be to Allah,' and 'Praise be to Allah.' That will be like food for them."

Mu'adh ibn Jabal reported that the Messenger of Allah, may Allah bless him and grant him peace, said, "The renaissance of Jerusalem will come when Yathrib is in ruins; the ruin of Yathrib will occur when fighting comes; the outbreak of fighting will be at the conquest of Constantinople; and the conquest of Constantinople will occur when the Dajjal appears." Then he struck his thigh or his shoulder with his hand and said, "This is as true as your presence here or as your sitting here (meaning that of Mu'adh ibn Jabal)." (al-Hakim and Abu Dawud)

Al-Mughira ibn Shu'ba reported, "No one asked the Prophet, may Allah bless him and grant him peace, more about the Dajjal than I did. He said, 'Why are you asking? He will not harm you.' I replied, 'They say that he will have mountains of bread and meat with him, and a river of water.' He replied, 'He is less significant in the sight of Allah for that.'" (Muslim)

Chapter Five

The Achievements of the Mahdi

The conquest of Constantinople

The Prophet, may Allah's peace and blessings be upon him, asked, "Have you heard of the city which has land on one side of it and sea on the other?" They replied, "Yes, Messenger of Allah." He said: "The Last Hour will not come before seventy thousand people of the descendants of Ishaq attack it. When they land there, they will neither fight with weapons nor shoot arrows but will only say: 'There is no god but Allah and Allah is greater', and the part of it facing the sea will fall. Then they will repeat again, 'There is no god but Allah, and Allah is greater', and its other side will fall. Then they will say, 'There is no god but Allah and Allah is greater' for the third time, and its gates will be opened for them and they will enter. They will be collecting spoils of war and distributing them among themselves when a cry will be heard: 'The Dajjal has come!' They will leave everything there and turn to (confront) him." (Muslim)

Abu Hurayra reported that the Messenger of Allah, may Allah bless him and grant him peace, said "The Last Hour will not come before the Romans land at al-A'maq or in Dabiq. An army consisting of the best of the people on Earth at that time will come from Madina to oppose them. When they deploy themselves in ranks, the Romans will say, 'Do not stand between us and those who took prisoners from among us. Let us fight them.' The Muslims will say, 'No, by Allah, we shall never turn aside from you or from our brothers so that you may fight them!'

"They will then fight and a third of the combatants, whom Allah will never forgive, will be routed. Another third, consisting

38

of excellent martyrs in Allah's eyes, will be killed. The last third, who will never experience temptation, will win and conquer Constantinople. While they are busy distributing the booty after hanging their swords from the olive trees, Shaytan will call out: 'The Dajjal has taken your place among your families!' They will then leave, and when they reach Syria he will appear while they are still preparing themselves for battle, drawing up the ranks.

"The time of prayer will come and then 'Isa ibn Maryam will descend and lead them in prayer. When the enemy of Allah sees him, he will melt away as salt dissolves in water. If 'Isa were to leave him he would melt away completely. But Allah will kill him by his hand and he will show them his blood on his spear." (Muslim)

The liberation of Jerusalem and unification of the world

The Almighty says:

> *"When the promised first time came, We sent against you slaves of Ours possessing great force, and they ransacked your houses, rampaging right through them, and it was a promise which was fulfilled."* (17:5)

> *"If you do good, you do it to your own selves. If you do evil, you do it against them. When the next promised time arrived, it was so that they could injure you and enter the Temple as they had entered it the first time, and in order to destroy completely what had been built."* (17:7)

The Prophet, may Allah bless him and grant him peace, said, "Prophethood will remain among you as long as Allah wishes it to remain, and then Allah will remove it when He wishes to remove it. Then there will be caliphate based on prophethood, and it will last as long as Allah wishes. Then Allah will remove it when He wishes. Then there will be a proud kingdom, and it will last as long as Allah wills. Then Allah will remove it when He wishes.

39

Then there will be caliphate based on prophethood." Then he was silent. (Ahmad at-Tayalisi, al-Bazzar and at-Tabarani: *sahih hadith*)

The prophethood referred to in the *hadith* is the mission of Muhammad, the Messenger of Allah, may Allah bless him and grant him peace. Then, after prophethood, came the rightly-guided caliphate: that of Abu Bakr, 'Umar, 'Uthman and 'Ali. After that came the inherited kingdom which brings us right up to the present impious unbelieving Masonic republics under whose sins, crime and malice towards Islam we are suffering today. Then, by the permission of Allah, the Mahdi will be victorious and eradicate those pigs and dogs and the idols of this time so that there will once more be caliphate based on prophethood as the *hadith* states.

Hudhayfa ibn al-Yaman said, "The people used to ask the Messenger of Allah, may Allah bless him and grant him peace, about good things but I used to ask about evil, fearing that it would reach me. I said, 'Messenger of Allah, we used to live in ignorance and evil. Then Allah brought us this good. Will there be evil after this good?' He replied, 'Yes.' I said, 'Will there be any good after that evil?' He said, 'Yes, but there will be murkiness in it.' I asked, 'What is that murkiness?' He said, 'People will follow guidance that is not my guidance. Some will be approved and some reprehensible.' I asked, 'Will there be any evil after that good?' He replied, 'Yes, those who call at the gates of Hell. Whoever responds to them and arrives at the gates will be thrown into it by them.' I asked, 'Messenger of Allah, describe them to us.' He replied, 'They are from our race and they will speak our language.' I asked, 'What do you command me to do if I am alive then?' He said, 'Cling to the community of the Muslims and their Imam.' I said, 'And if there is no community or Imam?' He replied, 'Then withdraw from all the sects, even if you have to cling to the root of a tree, until death takes you while you are in that condition.'"

Jerusalem will be the location of the rightly-guided caliphate and the centre of Islamic rule, which will be headed by Imam al-Mahdi. At the same time the Dajjal will be like a rapacious dog going around the world encouraging the Jews and the vile among the unbelievers and depraved women, hoping to occupy Jerusalem and be crowned as the 'Prince of Peace' in it. He will in fact return to be slain by a spear in the hand of 'Isa, who will be helped by the Mahdi on a day which will be known as the Day of Salvation when humanity will be delivered from the evil of the trials it is suffering from at the moment.

That will abolish the leadership of the Jews, who direct the world from within the Masonic circles, and put an end to the domination of the shaytans who spit evil into people and cause corruption in the earth, making them slaves of false idols and ruling the world by laws other than the *Shari'a* of the Lord of the worlds. It will be the Day of Salvation from this Era of Ignorance with the darkness, rancour and abasement of human beings which accompany it.

Chapter Six

Those who Pave the Way for the Mahdi

According to a *hadith* transmitted by Ahmad ibn Hanbal and Ibn Majah from Ibn Mas'ud, it was asked, "Messenger of Allah, who are the strangers?" He replied, "Those who leave their tribes." He was asked, "And who are they?" He replied, "Those who put matters right when people are corrupt."

Imam Ahmad reports in a *hadith* from Sa'd ibn Abi Waqqas, "Glad tidings for the strangers on that day!" and in others, "Those who flee with their *deen* from the tribulations." In one variant it says, "Those who hold to the Book when it is abandoned and teach my *Sunna* when it is neglected."

Abu Umayya ash-Sha'bani said, "I asked Abu Tha'laba about the words of the Almighty, *'O you who believe! You are responsible for yourselves alone. The misguided cannot harm you so long as you are guided. All of you will return to Allah and He will inform you about the things you did.'* (5:105) He replied, 'By Allah, I asked the one who was best informed about it. I asked the Messenger of Allah, who said, 'Command what is right and forbid what is wrong until you see avarice being obeyed, passion being followed, worldly interests being preferred and everyone being enamoured of their own opinion. Then look to yourself and leave alone what the majority of people are doing. For ahead of you there are days which will require steadfastness and in which holding to steadfastness will be like grasping live coals. He who acts rightly during that period will have the reward of fifty men.' He was asked, 'Messenger of Allah, the reward of fifty of us or fifty of them?' He replied, 'No, the reward of fifty of you.'"

These are the people who will prepare the way for the appearance of the Mahdi. They are strangers in the eye of the masses and the common people and in the eyes of the tyrants, terrorists and extremists. The real tyrants are the swine who betray Allah and His Messenger and their homelands by serving the False Messiah. They have Muslim names but are not Muslims in any true sense of the word.

> "We sent down the Torah containing guidance and light; and the Prophets who had submitted themselves gave judgement by it for the Jews, as did their scholars and their rabbis – by what they had managed to preserve of the Book of Allah and to which they were witnesses. Do not fear people, fear Me. And do not sell My signs for a paltry price. Those who do not judge by what Allah has sent down, they are the rejectors." (5:44)

The "strangers" are the people who prepare the way for the Mahdi, fighting in the Way of Allah with all the strength they possess to make the Word of Allah Almighty uppermost. Our Beloved Messenger Muhammad conveyed the good news of them: "A group of my Community will continue to fight for the Truth until 'Isa ibn Maryam descends at dawn in Jerusalem, He will descend to the Mahdi, who will tell him, 'Go forward, O Prophet of Allah, and lead us in the prayer.' He will say, 'This Community are leaders of one another as a mark of honour from Allah for them." (Al-Muqri)

The Black Banners

Thawban reported that the Messenger of Allah, may Allah bless him and grant him peace, said, "When you see the black banners coming from Khurasan, then go to them even if that means crawling over the snow. The Deputy of Allah, the Mahdi, will be among them."(Al-Hakim, ad-Dani, Nu'aym ibn Hammad, and as-Suyuti)

43

Muhammad ibn al-Hanafiyya said, "A banner will emerge from Khurasan and then some people will come out wearing white garments. At the head of them will be a man of the Banu Tamim paving the way for the rule of the Mahdi before he emerges, and he will hand over authority to the Mahdi after seventy-two months." (Al-Dani)

Thawban reported that the Messenger of Allah, may Allah bless him and grant him peace, said, "The Black Banners will come from the east and their hearts will be as firm as iron. Whoever hears about them should join them and give allegiance, even if that means crawling across snow." (Abu Nu'aym and as-Suyuti)

'Ali said, "The Sufyani and the Black Banners will meet at the gate of Istakhr (in Iran). Among them will be a youth from the Banu Hashim with a mole on his left hand and at the front will be a man of Banu Tamim called Shu'ayb ibn Salih. There will be a fierce battle between them; the Black Banners will be victorious and the cavalry of the Sufyani will flee. Then people will be adherants of the Mahdi and seek him out." (Nu'aym ibn Hammad)

It is related that 'Awf ibn Malik said, "I went to visit the Prophet, may Allah bless him and grant him peace, during the Tabuk expedition while he was in a leather tent. He said, 'Here are six signs which will indicate the approach of the Last Hour: my death; then the conquest of Jerusalem; then a plague which will carry you off like the pestilence of sheep; then the increase of wealth to such an extent that a man will be given a hundred dinars and still not be happy; then a trial which will not fail to enter every house of the Arabs; and then a truce between you and the Byzantines (Banu'l-Asfar) who will act treacherously and attack you under eighty flags with twelve thousand men under every flag.'" (al-Bukhari)

Those believers who are preparing the way for the Mahdi are selected men whom only Allah knows. They are hidden and god-fearing. When present they are not recognised. When absent they are not missed. They are not those young men of foolish dreams who contend in sects and voice their zeal, *each party exulting in*

44

what it has..." (23:53) except those among the Community of Muslims on whom Allah has mercy. In the same way the names of the tyrants who oppose the Mahdi are in reality attributes and descriptions, not actual names: some examples are al-Abqa (spotted)', al-Ashhab (grey), the Qahtani, the Jurhumi, the Sufyani and Kindite al-A'raj (lame man of Kinda), and so on.

Chapter Seven
The Trials Preceding the Mahdi

'Abdullah ibn Mas'ud said, "I heard the Messenger of Allah, may Allah bless him and grant him peace, say, 'There will be many trials and those who sleep through them will be better than those who lie down; those who lie down will be better than those who sit up; those who sit up will be better than those who stand up; those who stand up will be better than those who walk; those who walk will be better than those who ride; and those who ride will be better than those who run.' I said, 'Messenger of Allah, when will that be?' He said, 'Those will be the days of killing, when a man will not even be safe from his companion.' I asked, 'What do you command me to do if I am still alive in that time?' He said, 'Restrain yourself and your hand and enter your house.' I said, 'Messenger of Allah, what do you think I should do if some-one enters my house?' He said, 'Go to your room.' I said, 'What do you think I should do if someone enters my room?' He said, 'Go to your mosque and do such-and-such and hold their wrist and say, "My Lord is Allah," until you die in that condition.'" (al-Hakim, *al-Mustadrak*, with a sound *isnad*)

The stay-at-home trial

Abu Dawud related from 'Abdullah ibn 'Umar, "Once we were sitting with the Messenger of Allah, may Allah bless him and grant him peace, when he mentioned many of the trials which were to come. When he mentioned the trial during which people should stay at home and someone asked, 'Messenger of Allah, what is the stay-at-home trial?' He replied, 'It will be war and flight. Then a trial of prosperity will come which will be deceptive because it will be brought about by a man of my family who claims to be working for my cause when that is not the case. My friends are the godfearing. Then people will unite under a man who will be like a hip-bone on a rib. Then there will be a brief dark trial which will not fail to afflict everyone of this community – and then when people think it is finished it will start all over again. During it a man may be a believer in the morning and an unbeliever in the evening, and people will be in two camps: the camp of faith which will contain no hypocrisy, and the camp of hypocrisy which will contain no faith. When matters are like that, expect the Dajjal."

Few men of knowledge but many reciters

Abu Nu'aym stated in *al-Hilya,* quoting from a *hadith* of 'Abdullah ibn Mas'ud, that the Messenger of Allah, may Allah bless him and grant him peace, said, "How will you be when you are confused by a trial in which people adopt a custom whereby children have power and adults are weak and if you neglect it in any way you will be told that you have abandoned correct action?" People asked, "When will that be, Messenger of Allah?" He said, "When your reciters are many and your men of knowledge few, and your rulers are many and your trustworthy men few. And when you seek the wealth of this world by means of the actions of the Next World and learn *fiqh* other than for the sake of Allah."

This trial in which the mature will be weak and children strong will be a time when people claim to have knowledge. Every lad who studies will claim that he is holding to the *Sunna. Hadiths* will become weak and scholars will emerge who forge and show off. The knowledge of the great men of knowledge among the righteous will be deemed to be weak. This, by Allah, is what we see today among those of our youth who claim to have knowledge of *hadith.* They are deluded in their claim to knowledge. It is the result of having few men of real learning, many reciters and many self-styled leaders.

How many different factions there are! Each faction has a leader and this world has become the overriding concern of almost all of them. Students learn knowledge in order to obtain degrees for reputation and income. So people really do learn *fiqh* for the sake of other than Allah. This, by Allah, is what we see in our time. We ask Allah for safety and we hope that He will make us guided guides and resurrect us in the Company of the Righteous.

Usurious banks

Abu Dawud and Ibn Majah related from a *hadith* from Abu Hurayra that the Messenger of Allah said, may Allah bless him and grant him peace, "A time will come to mankind when there will not remain any people who do not consume usury. Those who do not actually consume it will be touched by its dust."

The spread of usury in the world is something evident which only an idiot would deny. The actions of the banks and their offshoots are undoubtedly based on the Jewish usury system and they empty into the golden vessels of the slaves of the Golden Calf, the followers of the myth of Zion. Even those who object to these banks are compelled to have dealings with them, like having salaries paid into them, using money orders, issuing cheques, and changing money. Everyone has to enter into some transactions which benefit the banks, thus touching the dust of usury, as the Truthful Confirmed Prophet, may Allah bless him and grant him peace, informed us. In spite of the fact that Allah has informed us that He has declared war on usury and curses usurers, the ignorant authorities in every place in the world pay not the slightest attention and have no shame whatsoever before Allah. That is why the world is full of misery, wars, plagues and wretchedness. Allah speaks the Truth:

> "*O you who believe! Fear Allah and forgo any remaining usury if you are believers. If you do not, know that it means war from Allah and His Messenger.*" (2:279)

Muslims should have as little to do with banks as possible since all dealings with them are unlawful. The Messenger of Allah, may Allah bless him and grant him peace, said, "Usury is equal to seventy sins, the least of which is a man's fornication with his mother." (al-Bayhaqi and Ibn Majah)

He also said, "Allah has cursed the consumer, the payer and the recorder of usury and those who refuse to pay *zakat*." (Ahmad and at-Tirmidhi)

Lack of trustworthiness

Abu Hurayra reported that a bedouin asked the Messenger of Allah, may Allah bless him and grant him peace, "When will the Last Hour come?" He replied, "When trustworthiness is lost then look for the Last Hour." He asked, "Messenger of Allah, how will it be lost?" He replied. "When authority is given to others than those who deserve it, then expect the Hour."

The authority referred to is that of the rightly-guided Caliphate of Allah which alone is able to achieve the rule of the Lord of the Worlds on earth, the diffusion of justice and peace and the light of Islam among people. This is the Trust which the heaven, earth and the mountains refused.

> *"We offered the Trust to the heavens and the earth and the mountains but they refused to take it on and were fearful of it. But man took it on. He is indeed wrongdoing and ignorant."* (33:72)

The contemporary situation of twentieth-century Ignorance affords proof of the complete abandonment of this Trust. Authority has been handed over to despicable people who do not rule by what Allah has revealed and do not make unlawful what Allah has made unlawful. So mankind has become miserable, downtrodden, and wronged because the rule of Shaytan is what governs them – not the judgement of the Wisest of Judges. That is why this matter is one of the signs of the Last Hour. Allah is enough for us, and how excellent a Guardian!

The abasement of the Arabs and Islam

Abu Musa reported that the Messenger of Allah, may Allah bless him and grant him peace, said, "I made supplication for the Arabs and said, 'O Allah! Whoever of them meets you acknowledging you, forgive him during his life.' This is the supplication of Ibrahim and Isma'il. On that Day the Banner of Praise will be in my Hand, and the closest of mankind to my banner on that day will be the Arabs." (al-Haythami, at-Tabarani)

It is a matter of honour and glory that the Qur'an was revealed in a clear Arabic tongue, and that the Master of Creation, Muhammad, the Messenger of Allah, may Allah bless him and grant him peace, was sent as one of the Arab race. This is the secret of the honour of the nation of Arabs and without it the Arabs are worthless. However Allah has placed a wisdom in it, for His Ancient House in Makka is the centre of the world and is located in the heart of the Arab nation which has forgotten and neglected this great honour. That is why the caliphate is reserved for the best stock of the Arabs – Quraysh – in order to preclude conflict over the responsibility and taking on the task whose burden the heavens and earth and mountains rejected and which will be a cause of evil and regret on the Day of Resurrection for anyone who does not fulfil it with fear of Allah.

If no Qurayshite can be found then anyone can be the caliph. The important thing is to establish the *deen* of Allah for Allah's sake alone. So it is a duty for this community to hold to the task of elevating the Word of Allah in the earth and not to waver from this *deen* until it leads and directs all humanity. Unfortunately, when the Arabs abandoned the Qur'an, made the unlawful lawful, and fell into the lap of the Europeans, they were abased and humiliated; and so Islam is abased. Jabir reported that the Messenger of Allah, may Allah bless him and grant him peace, said, "When the Arabs are abased, then Islam will be abased."

The estrangement of Islam

Abu Hurayra reported that the Prophet, may Allah bless him and grant him peace, said, "Islam began as something strange and will again become something strange as it began. Good news, then, for the strangers!" (Muslim, Ahmad and Ibn Majah) According to Ahmad and Ibn Majah, 'Abdullah ibn Mas'ud added, "Someone said, 'Messenger of Allah, who are the strangers?' He replied, 'Strangers to the tribes.'" In Ahmad, Sa'd ibn Abi Waqqas said, 'Joy to the strangers when people are corrupt."

Imam Ahmad and at-Tabarani quote a *hadith* of Ibn 'Umar from which says, "We asked, 'Who are the strangers, Messenger of Allah?' He replied, 'A few people among many evil people. Those who disobey them are far more numerous than those who obey them.'"

The contemporary situation is rife with injustice, tyranny, corruption and human misery. The Muslim drowning in this ocean of miseries and tragedies is bewildered and wretched. He can find no refuge to which to flee with his *deen* and rushes from precipice to precipice. He bears the hardship of life in forests beset by wolves, vipers and scorpions. Whenever he strives to proclaim the Truth, people accuse him and plot against him. He becomes a stranger in his own land and among his own people and tribe, simply by holding to Allah's *deen* and desiring the best for mankind. The entire world schemes against him by night and day when all he is doing is calling people to the goal of fulfilling their highest potential: the worship of their Lord Who has no need of them. People suspect of him being a reactionary, an extremist, and a terrorist. The truth is that they are the backward ones and the wrongdoers. The worst thing is that some of them call themselves Muslims and claim to be part of the Community of Muhammad, may Allah bless him and grant him peace!

How can that be the case when they attack the Qur'an, govern by the laws of the Jews and Christians, make lawful what Allah has made unlawful and unlawful what He has made lawful, and take the unbelievers as friends and fight the righteous? They are corrupt criminals, agents and slaves of the Masons, rulers of the world who do not raise the banner of *tawhid* or judge by what Allah has revealed!

Refusal to judge by what Allah has revealed

'Abdullah ibn 'Amr ibn al-'As reported that he heard the Messenger of Allah, may Allah bless him and grant him peace, say, "The Last Hour will not come before Allah takes His *Shari'a* away from the people of the earth, leaving no one in it but heathens who do not recognise right or object to wrong."

Everywhere on earth the Qur'an has been abandoned and its judgements rejected. Nowhere is the *Shari'a* properly applied and the unlawful completely prohibited. Right has been made wrong and wrong right. The strange thing is that you find people claiming to love Allah and His Book and His Prophet, may Allah bless him and grant him peace, when they persist in deviance and disobedience and cast aside the decrees of the Qur'an. They judge by man-made laws and suffer accordingly. They have lost their way. They find themselves abased by the courts and dishonoured in police cells. All of that comes from following leaders who rule by other than what Allah has revealed. Allah speaks the truth:

> *"Do you not see those who claim that they believe in what has been revealed to you and what was revealed before you, still desiring to turn to a satanic source for judgement in spite of being commanded to reject it? Shaytan wants to misguide them far away."* (4:60)

> *"Those who do not judge according to what Allah has revealed, they are the unjust."* (5:45)

Skyscrapers, the shortening of time and many earthquakes

Al-Bukhari related in his *Sahih* collection from Abu Hurayra that the Messenger of Allah, may Allah bless him and grant him peace, said, "The Last Hour will not come before knowledge is removed, there are many earthquakes, time passes quickly, trials appear and people build tall buildings."

At-Tirmidhi quotes from a *hadith* of Anas ibn Malik in which the Messenger of Allah, may Allah bless him and grant him peace, said: "The Last Hour will not come before time passes quickly and a year is like a month, a month like a week, a week like a day, a day like an hour, and an hour like the flickering of a flame."

At-Tabari related from Abu Musa al-Ash'ari that the Messenger of Allah, may Allah bless him and grant him peace, said, "The Last Hour will not come before time passes quickly and the earth is rolled up (meaning distances are made to seem shorter)."

In the *Sahih* collection of al-Bukhari, Abu Hurayra reports that the Messenger of Allah, may Allah bless him and grant him peace said, "Time will pass quickly and knowledge will be lost." One variant has, "And action will be lost, avarice will be common and there will be much killing."

Who among us is not aware of the swift passage of time? By Allah, not a day passes but it appears as if people get out of bed and there are only a few fleeting moments before they get back into it again. It will continue like that until time accelerates to the point that a year is like a month, a month like a week, a week like a day, a day like an hour, and an hour like the flickering of a flame. Glory be to Allah! There is no blessing in the moment at all! We ask Allah for mercy. Similarly, the Final Hour is not destined to arrive until civil unrest and trials are numerous; but now we are living through a time when this is manifestly the case. We hope for deliverance from them. One of these afflictions is the disappearance of knowledge.

Imitation of the West

Al-Bukhari related from Abu Sa'id al-Khudri that the Messenger of Allah, may Allah bless him and grant him peace, said: "You will follow the custom of those before you span by span and cubit by cubit to the point that if they were to go down a lizard's hole you would follow them." Someone asked: 'The Jews and the Christians, Messenger of Allah?" He replied, "Them."

Al-Bazzar and al-Hakim related from a *hadith* from Ibn 'Abbas that the Messenger of Allah, may Allah bless him and grant him peace, said, "You will follow the customs of those before you inch by inch and span by span and cubit by cubit, to the point that if one of them were to go down a lizard's hole you too would enter it. Even if one of them were to have intercourse with his mother, you would do it."

At-Tabarani related that Ibn Mas'ud reported that the Messenger of Allah, may Allah bless him and grant him peace, said, "You are like the nations of the tribe of Israel and you will follow their path step by step until there is nothing they have that you do not have as well, to the point that people will be approached by a woman and one of them will go to her and lie with her and then return to his friends and laugh with them."

No one travelling through the countries known as 'Muslim lands' can help but notice that the European arena seems to have moved from Piccadilly and Montmartre to Tangier, Tunis, Cairo and Damascus. Men are like women and women are devoid of modesty, blatantly displaying their charms. Frequently the sexes resemble one other to the extent that you are forced to ask yourself, "Is this a man or a woman?" Things have reached the point where such vileness is perpetrated that the situation which the Prophet, may Allah bless him and grant him peace, told us about has become commonplace.

The odd thing, and something which is an absolute proof of backwardness and intellectual barrenness, is that we find Muslim writers and thinkers researching, debating, arguing and competing to join the mad rush to "progress and advancement" as represented by the Western societies whose hallmark is sexual licence, moral disintegration and family dysfunctionality. Shaytan has succeeded in making them imagine that the Jews and Christians in the West are the true representatives of humanity and civilisation, while the Muslims appear to them to be backward and devoid of culture.

The Muslims must beware of blind imitation. It is honour enough for them to follow and imitate the noblest of Creation, Muhammad, may Allah bless him and grant him peace. Allah speaks the truth:

"You have an excellent model in the Messenger of Allah, for all who put their hope in Allah and the Last Day."

(33:21)

Women who are clothed yet naked

Muslim related in his *Sahih* collection from Abu Hurayra that the Messenger of Allah, may Allah bless him and grant him peace, said, "There are two types of people of the Fire whom I have not seen: people who have whips like oxtails with which they beat people, and women who are clothed yet naked, with hair piled high like the humps of camels, who are inclined (to evil) and make their husbands incline towards it. They will not enter the Garden or even smell its scent although its scent can be smelled at such-and-such a distance."

Ahmad related in his *Musnad* from 'Abdullah ibn 'Amr ibn al-'As that the Messenger of Allah, may Allah bless him and grant him peace, said, "In the last days of my Community there will be men who ride on saddles who resemble the men who dismount at the doors of the mosques. Their women will be clothed yet naked with their hair piled high on their heads like lean camel humps. Curse them! Truly they are accursed."

The tyrants and despots who do not judge by the laws of the Qur'an or respect what Allah and His Messenger have made unlawful have forces who control people with whips and cudgels which resemble the tails of cattle. Those police who are the servants of tyrants are the dogs of the fire because they help those rulers who govern by other than what Allah has sent down and they work to serve them and support their unjust power. To further the transgression and opposition to the truth of this time, made-up women play a role through their corrupting influence. One aspect of that corruption are the sheer garments they wear so that they can honestly be described as being clothed yet naked. That is why the Messenger of Allah, did not say 'clothed **and** naked', but 'clothed **yet** naked', meaning that they wear clothes which do not really cover their bodies but make them appear as if they were naked. This style of dress has now spread throughout the world and you will even see women emerging from mosques wearing such clothes. They walk leaning over from the effect of tight clothes and high-heeled shoes. Such women uncover their hair and have it elaborately styled at the hairdressers so their heads really do resemble the humps of camels.

Killer aeroplanes and the terror they inspire

'Abdu'r-Razzaq related, "Woe to the Arabs because of an evil which has drawn near. Wings! What wings! Long woe in the wings that have a wind in which they move, a wind generated by their movement and a wind emerging from the sides by their movement." (*al-Musannaf*, 11:352)

Arab concern about cultural backwardness and scientific under-development is the result of propaganda put out by the unbelievers against the establishment of the Islamic state which in reality represents the peak of justice, progress, civilisation and advancement. The Muslims seek to imitate the West because of their military superiority which has given them the power to intimidate and threaten other nations. Their principal weapons of destruction are the aeroplanes which the Master of Creation, may Allah bless him and grant him peace, described as having long woe in their wings; and it is a fact that aeroplanes carry their missiles and destructive bombs beneath their wings. The secret of air flight is air power which creates a powerful wind. Glory be to Allah!

Recording machines, spying devices and wild beasts speaking

Ahmad reported in his *Musnad* from a *hadith* from Abu Sa'id al-Khudri that the Messenger of Allah, may Allah bless him and grant him peace, said, "By the One who has my soul in His hand, the Last Hour will not come before animals speak to people or before the strap of a man's whip and the strap of his sandal speak and tell him what people have said after he has gone." (at-Tirmidhi as *hasan sahih gharib*; al-Hakim)

According to other sources, Abu Hurayra related that the Prophet said: "There are signs before the Last Hour, to the point that a man will go out and when he returns his sandals and whip will speak to him about what people have said in his absence."

We live in the fifteenth century *Hijri* in an age when scientific progress and electronics have reached the point where a man can place a small recording device looking like a pen or even a sandal or a whip to record what people say in his absence. It is now even possible for what happened in his absence to be filmed on video using small cameras which record both people's words and their actions. As for the speaking of animals, there have already been some examples of that happening.

The elimination of men of knowledge

'Abdullah ibn 'Umar reported that he heard the Prophet, may Allah bless him and grant him peace, say, "Allah will not remove knowledge after He has given it to you by wrenching it away (from hearts). He will remove it from you by removing the men of knowledge along with their knowledge, so that only ignorant people will remain; people will seek their opinion and they will be misguided and misguide others." (al-Bukhari)

Only the Qur'an and the *Sunna are* true knowledge and it is through the efforts of the sincere men of knowledge of this Community who study and explain them clearly and correctly that people understand the fundamentals of their *deen* and its laws and obligations and duties. This knowledge will never be removed because Islam is the *deen* of Allah and the final concluding Message. It is the truth and what is other than it is false. The men of knowledge fight in the struggle between disbelief and belief. The forces of evil, lies and injustice are set against the men of knowledge and are determined to suppress them. Some are killed, others are imprisoned, and others are forced to conceal their belief.

"For if they find out about you, they will stone you or make you revert to their religion and then you will never have success." (18:20)

The upshot is that real men of knowledge are stifled and those who remain are in fact agents and supporters of the authorities, scholars of evil, cowards who are the servants and upholders of unjust rulers. They declare things lawful for them and give them their fill of the unlawful and make friends with the enemies of Allah and slander the Community. How many obligations like *jihad* and campaigns for the Cause of Allah, commanding right and forbidding wrong have been forgotten, leading people to imagine that Islam is merely a personal religion consisting of prayer, fasting, marriage and divorce! No caliphate or governance is established anywhere. It is as if Islam were simply a matter of ancient history.

The good qualities of the Europeans

Mustawrid al-Qurashi said that he heard the Messenger of Allah, may Allah bless him and grant him peace, say, "The Last Hour will come when the majority of people are Romans." 'Amr ibn al-'As told him, "Think what you are saying!" He said, "I only say what I heard from the Messenger of Allah, may Allah bless him and grant him peace." 'Amr replied: "If you say that, it is a fact; for they have four qualities. They are the most controlled of people under trial. They are swift in recovering after a calamity. They attack again after fleeing. They have (the quality of) being good to the destitute, orphans, and the weak; and, fifthly, an excellent trait they have is that they put up resistance to the injustice of kings." (Muslim)

By Allah, we can see certain confirmation of this. "The Romans" means the Europeans, and it is now certainly true that the Europeans and their imitators are the most numerous people on the earth. The Chosen Prophet spoke the truth, may Allah bless him and grant him peace. In spite of their disbelief, plotting and rancour towards Islam, they do undoubtedly possesses the good qualities mentioned. Under trial they do not act irresponsibly but exercise self-restraint. This is why we find that they are methodical and orderly people. When they are afflicted by a calamity they do not give up. It is as if the difficulty had never occurred. They are cowards but less cowardly than the Jews. When they flee they come back again. They love the destitute, orphans and the weak. This is why we find that they set up charitable missions but they have an evangelistic aim. They detest injustice and put up the strongest resistance to the injustice of rulers.

The contemptible, lowly and noble

Ahmad, Abu Ya'la, at-Tahawi and at-Tabarani related from Anas ibn Malik that the Messenger of Allah, may Allah bless him and grant him peace, declared, "Before the Last Hour there will be years of deceit in which liars will be believed and the truthful will be thought liars, the treacherous will be trusted and the trustworthy thought treacherous, and in which the contemptible will speak." He was asked, "What is meant by 'the contemptible'?" He replied, "Unrighteous people who speak about public affairs."

Al-Bazzar and at-Thawri reported the same thing from 'Umar ibn 'Awf, with the difference that when the Messenger of Allah was asked, "What is meant by 'the contemptible'?" he replied, "Wicked leaders who speak about public affairs."

At-Tahawi said, "It was asked 'What is meant by the contemptible, Messenger of Allah?' and he replied, 'Those who are worthless.'" That is how at-Tabarani reported it from a *hadith* narated by 'Awf ibn Malik. Ash-Shafi'i reported it from Abu Hurayra who narrated that the Messenger of Allah, may Allah bless him and grant him peace, said: "Years of deceit will come to people during which liars are believed and the truthful thought liars, and the treacherous are trusted and the trustworthy thought treacherous, and in which the contemptible will speak." He was asked, "Who are the contemptible?" He said, "Unrighteous men who speak about public affairs"

At-Tabari reported from Abu Hurayra that the Messenger of Allah, may Allah bless him and grant him peace, said, "By the One who has my soul in His hand, the Last Hour will not come before shamelessness and miserliness are commonplace and the trustworthy are mistrusted and the treacherous trusted, and the noble destroyed and the lowly triumphant." They asked, "Messenger of Allah, who are the noble and who are the lowly?" He replied, "The noble are the true leaders and significant people and the lowly are those who are under the feet of the people and are unknown."

The Masonic movement throughout the world is like a viper with multiple heads and tails which appear everywhere and which aims its venom with utter enmity towards Islam and Muslims. For the implementation of its plans it chooses only the wicked who are devoted to it – those who are eager for worldly wealth and desperate for rank and position because they are low and deprived under the feet of their Jewish masters.

I am speaking the truth when I say that the slaves of the Masons are those about whom the Messenger of Allah was speaking, may Allah bless him and grant him peace. They are the lowly and contemptible, serving those base tyrants who have no lineage, *deen* or honour. You see them speaking about the affairs of the world. The nobles are the rightful masters of people and they have been eliminated. That is what we now see as a political, social and cultural fact in the world.

Unbelievers reciting the Qur'an

Ibn 'Abbas reported that the Messenger of Allah, may Allah bless him and grant him peace, said, "The Qur'an will be read by people of my Community who pass through Islam as an arrow passes through game." (Ahmad ibn Hanbal)

Throughout the history of Islam after the death of the fourth caliph, 'Ali, may Allah be pleased with him, there have appeared sects, splinter groups and groups beyond the pale of Islam. Early on there was the appearance of the imposters Sajah and Musaylima who claimed prophethood and each one had a logical line of thought which underpinned and supported his satanic course.

Later on other groups appeared like the Qaramatians, the 'Alawites, the Kharijites and Murji'ites. Things continued like this until the appearance this century of the Qadiyanis, Bahais, secularists, missionaries and other misleading parties which are simply continuations of the ancient apostate sects and beliefs which split from Islam early on, although all claim to be Muslims and recite the Qur'an. Indeed, the situation has now reached the point where modern reciters are simply the servants of the tyrants, supporters of ignorant governments. They love the tyrants who persist in disobedience to Allah, supporting them in their devotion to reprehensible deeds – with the rare exception of those on whom Allah has mercy and whom Allah has preserved from passing through the *deen* as the arrow passes through game. We ask Allah for safety!

Reversion to idolatry

Abu Hurayra reported that the Messenger of Allah, may Allah bless him and grant him peace, said, "The Last Hour will not come until the buttocks of the women of the tribe of Daws shake around Dhu'l-Khulaysa, the idol of Daws whom they used to worship in the *Jahiliyya*."

'A'isha reported that she heard the Messenger of Allah say, may Allah bless him and grant him peace, "Night and day will not

61

depart before al-Lat and al-'Uzza are worshipped again." She said, "Messenger of Allah, I thought that when Allah revealed *'It is He who sent His Messenger with the Guidance and the* Deen *of Truth to exalt it over every other* deen, *even though the idolaters hate it,'* (9:33) the business was complete." He replied, may Allah bless him and grant him peace, "That will apply to those whom Allah wills. He will send a sweet breeze which will cause all who have the weight of a grain of mustard seed of belief in his heart to die; and the only people left will be those who have no good in them; and they will revert to the *deen* of their forefathers."

By Allah, I have seen with my own eyes and touched with my own hands the idols of the tyrants which people worship instead of Allah. I have heard with my own ears about Ataturk who completely transformed Turkey and fought Islam by every criminal means he could to such a point that they reverence his icons instead of Allah. These icons are set up everywhere in Turkey, even in the mosques. The same thing has happened with pictures of Saddam Husayn and other rulers who are revered instead of Allah. This is the case with all our rulers who do not rule by what Allah has revealed or make unlawful what Allah has made unlawful.

The prophecy of the Prophet must come true and it is clear that these idols of the tyrants are nothing more than the beginning of a return by the dregs of mankind to the worship of al-Lat and al-'Uzza and Dhu'l-Khulaysa. People will be seen acting in accordance with what the Prophet said about the buttocks of the women of Daws shaking around the idol Dhu'l-Khulaysa. That is due to the gradual distancing of people from their *deen* which is the object of the Masonic plan that we see coming to fruition today. It will reach the point where the ancient idols of al-Lat and al-'Uzza are worshipped once more.

Abundance of wealth and women

Abu Musa al-Ash'ari reported that the Messenger of Allah, may Allah bless him and grant him peace, said, "A time will come to people when a man will go around with his *sadaqa* of gold and not find anyone to take it from him, and when a man will be seen followed by forty women seeking refuge with him because of the shortage of men and the abundance of women." (al-Bukhari)

Anas reported that the Messenger of Allah, may Allah bless him and grant him peace, said, "One of the signs of the Last Hour is that knowledge will be removed and there will be much ignorance and much fornication and wine will be drunk. There will be so many women that one man will have fifty women in his charge." (al-Bukhari)

Abu Hurayra reported that the Messenger of Allah, may Allah bless him and grant him peace, said, "The Last Hour will not come before there is much wealth among you. It will overflow to the point the owner of wealth will be worried about who will accept his *sadaqa* and until the person to whom he offers it says, 'No, I have no need of it.'" (al-Bukhari and Muslim)

However much the world economy has improved, the point has not yet been reached where a man can go out with his *sadaqa* and not find anyone to take it. But that will happen and the time will come when the earth will reach that state. We ask Allah for pardon and deliverance!

Together with the tribulations concerning money come those of women, the spread of alcohol consumption, the disapperace of knowledge, the great number of ignorant men, the spread of fornication, and a great number of wars so that men will be so few, because of being killed in battle, that one man will have forty women under his protection, turning to him and contending for him because of the small number of men. All of these things will happen.

Earthquakes due to fornication, music and wine

Abu Malik al-Ash'ari reported that the Messenger of Allah, may Allah bless him and grant him peace, said, "People of my community will drink wine and call it something else; musical

63

instruments will be played for them and singers will sing. Allah will cause the earth to swallow them up and will make monkeys and pigs of them." (Ibn Majah)

'A'isha was asked about earthquakes and said, "If a woman removes her clothes in a house other than her husband's, she tears down the veil between herself and Allah. If she puts on perfume for anyone other than her husband, it is fire and disgrace for her. When fornication is made lawful and after this wine is drunk and musical instruments played, Allah will be jealous in His Heaven and will say to the earth, 'Make them tremble!' If they repent and stop, then all will be well. Otherwise it will crash down with them." (al-Hakim)

By Allah, we have lived through that and worse. Wine has been made lawful and given other names like whisky, vodka, beer and champagne. It is even produced in countries which are supposedly Muslim and whose leaders have Muslim names. Fornication has been made lawful and there is official licence for it in certain districts or else it exists under the cover of night-clubs and cabarets. Women go out made up to the hilt with no shame of Allah or anyone else. It is a shameful fact that the false leaders allow the shores of their countries to be flooded with women who are all but naked. Men and women are totally mixed together and there is no jealousy or modesty or fear of Allah.

Fornication in the middle of the road

The Prophet, may Allah bless him and grant him peace, said, "A man will go to a woman and lie with her in the road or will lift her skirt as the tail of a sheep is lifted. The best and most excellent of people on that day will be those who say, 'If you would only conceal yourselves behind that wall.' In that time such a man will be like Abu Bakr and 'Umar." (Abu Ya'la)

We belong to Allah and to Him we return! There is no strength or power except with Allah! This is the state of humanity now, except for those on whom Allah has mercy. Fornication can be bought in many areas of the world and it has even begun to be practised in the middle of the road. There are districts where it is allowed in Iraq, Morocco, and Lebanon and many other so-called Muslim countries. It was openly allowed for some decades in Egypt, Aden, Sudan, Algeria and Tunisia during the colonial period and after they departed the colonial powers left deputies and agents who are simply their slaves. They still do not rule by the *Shari'a* of the Qur'an. The most godfearing people are those who do their best to screen the corruption out of zeal for the prohibitions of Allah.

Desire for death

Abu Hurayra reported that the Messenger of Allah, may Allah bless him and grant him peace, said, "This world will not end before a man passes by a grave and rolls on it and says, 'O would that I were in the place of this person in the grave! The *deen* is nothing but affliction.'"

Abu Dharr said, "The time has almost come when a funeral will pass by a group of people in a market and a man will see it and shake his head and say, 'O would that I were in his place!'" He was asked, "O Abu Dharr, is that because of something terrible?" He said, "Yes."

The terrors of these terrible and intense trials and extraordinary events will bewilder even the most forbearing of people. How often do we now hear men and women wishing for death out of fear of the vicissitudes of present day life or to escape their cares and worries! People hope to die to be relieved of the toils of this world and its temptations. How many Muslims envy the place of those in the grave, desiring death not so much out of despair as out of fear and dislike of this world and the corruption in it!

Ibn Battal said, "The people in the graves will be envied and death will desired when the great trials appear. That is due to fear of the end of the world on account of the prevalence of falsehood, the corruption of its people, and the appearance of disobedience and evil."

65

Glory be to Allah! If Ibn Battal had seen our time and the trials we face and the estrangement of Islam in it and the persecution of the people of belief! It can only be that the Hour is drawing near. All we can do is say, "O Allah, make me die when death is better for me in my *deen* and my life and the end of my affair and make me live as long as life is good for me in my end, my life and the end of my affair."

Insincerity in the *Hajj*

Ibn 'Abbas reported that the Messenger of Allah, may Allah bless him and grant him peace, said, "O Salman, when kings make *Hajj* for the sake of pleasure, the rich for the sake of commerce, the poor for the sake of begging, and reciters for the sake of showing-off and reputation, then the star with a tail will soon appear." (Ibn Mardawayh)

By Allah, it is as the truthful Prophet said, and all anyone needs to do to be certain of it is to go on *Hajj*. The kings and leaders of this time go on *Hajj* as a diversion, staying in palaces and enjoying comfort and ease when the *Hajj* is a matter of hardship and effort and endurance. They treat *Hajj* as a holiday. As for wealthy businessmen, all you have to do is look at their suitcases bulging with goods. You find them going on *Hajj* every year not out of desire for the reward but out of greed for wealth and commerce. You see the poor and wretched begging and asking people for dirhams and dinars. And it is abundantly clear that reciters and scholars often go seeking livelihood and reputation except for the few on whom Allah shows mercy.

Lack of humility in the prayer and the appearance of innovators

Hudhayfa said, "The first thing to go missing from your *deen* will be humility and the last thing will be the prayer itself. Islam will be shrivelled up bit by bit. Women will pray while they are menstruating and you will travel the path of those before you exactly, step by step and point by point. Do not follow their path and follow their error. It will reach a point where two groups remain and one says, 'What is the point of the five prayers? Those before us were misguided. Allah Almighty says, *"Establish the prayer at the two ends of the day and in the first part of the night."* (11:114) There are only three prayers!' The other group will say, 'The belief of those who believe in Allah is like the belief of the angels. There is no unbeliever or hypocrite among us.' It is the right of Allah to gather them with the Dajjal." (al-Hakim)

Who among those of us who pray is not aware of those who fidget and play about in the prayer as if they were plagued by lice and fleas, thus showing no humility in their prayer? We seek refuge with Allah!

As for abandoning the prayer without excuse, how many so-called Muslims with Muslim names do not pray even though they know the words of the Almighty, *"Establish the prayer and do not be among the idolaters."* The Prophet, may Allah bless him and grant him peace, stated, "The contract between us and them is the prayer. Whoever abandons it has disbelieved."

There is also a group who says that none of them are hypocrites or unbelievers. Another group says that they will pray only *Fajr* and *'Isha'*, because Iblis has confused them.

The mountain of gold in the Euphrates

Al-Bukhari reports from Abu Hurayra that the Messenger of Allah, may Allah bless him and grant him peace, said, "The time has almost come when the Euphrates will uncover a treasure of gold. Whoever is present should not take any of it."

Muslim reported in his *Sahih* from Abu Hurayra, "The Last Hour will not come before the Euphrates uncovers a mountain of gold over which people will fight and ninety-nine of every hundred will be killed."

The Euphrates is a river which flows through Syria and Iraq with its sister, the Tigris. They eventually meet and empty into the Gulf. The Final Hour will not come before the Euphrates uncovers a mountain of gold over which people will fight and vast numbers will be killed. Muslims should not have anything to do with it. As for how this gold mountain will be uncovered, Allah knows best. The waters of the Euphrates may decrease and there will be a mountain in the heart of the river which will be uncovered. Or it may appear through explosives and modern excavation. Perhaps it is black gold (oil) which is referred to. We ask Allah for deliverance.

Rarity of true brotherhood, lawful dirhams and useful knowledge

Ibn 'Umar reported that the Messenger of Allah, may Allah bless him and grant him peace, said, "The rarest things in existence at the end of time will be a dirham from what is lawful and a brother who can be trusted." (Abu Nu'aym)

Something similar is related by Abu Nu'aym and at-Tabarani: "A time will come on you in which there is nothing harder to come by than three things: a brother with whom you are intimate, a dirham of the lawful or a *sunna* which is acted upon.'"

Hudhayfa reported that the Messenger of Allah, may Allah bless him and grant him peace, said, "The Last Hour will not come before Allah makes three things rare: a dirham of the lawful, useful knowledge, and a brother in Allah." (*Kanz al-'Ummal*)

The appearance of bad characteristics among the Muslims

'Ali ibn Abi Talib reported that the Messenger of Allah, may Allah bless him and grant him peace, said, "When my Community has fifteen characteristics, affliction will become lawful for them."

He was asked, "What are they, Messenger of Allah?" He said, "When booty is taken in turn (by particular groups), property given in trust is treated as booty, *zakat* is thought of as a fine, a man obeys his wife and disobeys his mother, a man is amiable to his friend and harsh to his father, voices are raised in mosques, the leader of a people is the worst of them, a man is honoured out of fear of the evil he can do, wine is drunk, silk is worn, singers and stringed instruments appear, and the last of this Community curse the first. At that time look for a violent wind or the earth opening up or transmogrification." (at-Tirmidhi)

AIDS and other afflictions

'Ata' ibn Abi Rabah said, "We were with Ibn 'Umar when a young man of Basra came and asked about something and he said, 'Shall I inform you about that?' He said, 'Once there were ten of us with the Messenger of Allah, may Allah bless him and grant him peace, in the mosque of the Messenger of Allah: Abu Bakr, 'Umar, 'Uthman, 'Ali, Ibn Mas'ud, Hudhayfa, Abu Sa'id al-Khudri, another man, and myself, when a young man of the Ansar came and greeted the Messenger of Allah, may Allah bless him and grant him peace, and then stood there and said, "Messenger of Allah, which believers are best?" He said, "Those who have the best character." He asked, "Which believers are the shrewdest?" He replied, "Those who remember death most and prepare for it most thoroughly before it comes to them."

"'Then the lad was silent and the Messenger of Allah turned to us and said, "Whenever fornication appears among a people, plagues and famine appear among them which were not known to their ancestors. When they give short measure and weight, they are afflicted by drought, intense trouble and tyranny from those who rule them. When they refuse to pay the *zakat* due on their property, they are denied rain from Heaven, and were it not for the animals, it would not rain at all. When they break the contract of Allah and the contract of His Messenger, their enemy is given power over them and takes some of what is in their hands. When their Imams fail to judge by the Book of Allah, Allah makes them harm one another.'" This is what we now see. The Prophet, may Allah bless him and grant him peace, spoke the truth.

Epilogue

From the preceding material, and the quite graphically specific nature of much of it, it may seem evident that many of the signs and trials referred to are already upon us and therefore that the time of the Mahdi is indeed very close. This makes it all the more necessary to add a cautionary note at this point. The Muslims must not allow the seeming dominance of the unbelievers and anticipatory longing for the arrival of the Mahdi to overwhelm them and make them despair of establishing the *deen* or to induce passivity, fatalism and quietism in them. Allah commands the Muslims in His Book never to give up the fight to establish His *deen*.

> *"Fight them until idolatry is no more and the* deen *is Allah's alone."* (2:192)

> *"Fight them until idolatry is no more and the* deen *is completely Allah's alone."* (8:39)

If the Muslims give up struggling to implement Islam they will simply be playing into the hands of the enemies of Islam who, being well-aware of the longing of the Muslims for the Mahdi, have long been determined to exploit this for their own ends to undermine *jihad* and to keep the Muslims quiescent. The colonialist powers made use of Mahdism to keep their subject populations passive and those who have taken over from them encourage the same attitude whenever possible. A Dutch orientalist put the whole policy very succinctly at the end of the last century:

> Finally it (Islam) will have to yield: it must abandon the doctrine of *jihad* and partly transfer it to the practically harmless doctrine regarding the end of the world, the

Messianic or Mahdist expectations ... Before it comes to that, however, the last political centre of Islam will probably have been brought under European influence, and all less civilised Mohammadan peoples must have learnt to submit to a strong European rule. (C. Snock Hurgronje, *De Atjehers*)

The Muslims must not allow themselves to become the dupes of their declared enemies; and they should also remember that, as has been made clear in this book, the Dajjal has vast numbers of weak Muslims among his followers. Only those Muslims who hold very firmly to the path left by the Prophet and his Companions, whose lives were all spent in the uncompromising struggle to see Allah's *deen* established in all its fullness on earth, will be safe from him. We seek refuge with Allah! So while it seems clear that the time is near, the Muslims must drop neither their guard nor their determination. The best preparation for the coming of the Mahdi can only be *"to fight to the utmost for Allah as He deserves to be fought for."* (22:78) We must remember the Prophet's instructions to us that if we are planting a tree when the Last Day arrives we should continue to do it. What tree could be nobler than the Tree of Islam?

So we must not despair and deny the existence of the Mahdi simply because he has not yet appeared, nor must we spend our lives waiting passively for his arrival. As in all things, we must keep a balanced perspective, using the discrimination with which our noble Prophet, may Allah bless him and grant him peace, has given us and which has been made so clear to us in the pages of this book.

Index